ELT Development Series

SERIES EDITOR Thomas S. C. Farrell

T0382680

REVISED EDITION

Teaching Reading

Richard Day

tesol press

www.tesol.org/bookstore

TESOL International Association
1925 Ballenger Avenue
Alexandria, Virginia, 22314 USA
www.tesol.org

Director of Publishing and Product Development: Myrna Jacobs
Copy Editor: Meg Moss
Production Editor: Kari S. Dalton
Cover Design: Citrine Sky Design
Interior Design and Layout: Capitol Communications, LLC

ISBN 9781945351785
eBook ISBN 9781945351792
Library of Congress Control Number 2019956803

Table of Contents

Part IV: Reading Comprehension

Part V: Key Considerations

Series Editor's Preface

The *English Language Teacher Development (ELTD)* series consists of a set of short resource books for ESL/EFL teachers that are written in a jargon-free and accessible manner for all types of teachers of English (native, nonnative, experienced, and novice). The ELTD series is designed to offer teachers a theory-to-practice approach to second language teaching, and each book presents a wide variety of practical approaches to and methods of teaching the topic at hand. Each book also offers reflections to help teachers interact with the materials presented. The books can be used in preservice settings or in in-service courses and by individuals looking for ways to refresh their practice. Now, after nearly 10 years in print, the ELTD series presents newly updated, revised editions that are even more dynamic than their first editions. Each of these revised books has an expanded number of chapters, as well as updated references from which various activities have been drawn and lesson plans for teachers to consider.

Richard Day's revised edition of *Teaching Reading* again explores different approaches to teaching reading in second language classrooms. Five new short chapters have been added: "Intensive Reading," "Comprehension Activities," "Reading and Vocabulary," "Selecting a Reading Textbook," and "Assessing Reading." The author has also added a lesson plan to the chapter "Planning the Reading Lesson." As he notes, the overarching goal of this book is to engage teachers in reflection on how reading may be taught to ESOL learners, and this revised edition is again a valuable addition to the literature in our profession.

I am very grateful to the authors of the ELTD series for sharing their knowledge and expertise with other TESOL professionals to make these short books affordable for all language teachers throughout the world. It is truly an honor for me to work again with each of these authors for the advancement of TESOL.

Thomas S. C. Farrell

CHAPTER 1

What Is Reading?

One way to introduce the nature of reading is to directly engage the reader (you) and to ask you to think about what you are doing, mentally, as you read this sentence. So stop reading, look away from the page, and think about the act of reading, what you did when you read this paragraph, and complete this sentence:

REFLECTIVE QUESTION

● Complete this sentence:
— Reading is _____.

Your answer most likely had something to do with comprehension, with meaning, and with understanding. This is the most common way that people think of reading. This view of reading as comprehension is generally thought of as a cognitive or mental view of reading—of what takes place in the brains. A useful cognitive definition is this:

Reading comprises a number of interactive processes between the reader and the text during which the reader uses his or her knowledge to build, to create, and to construct meaning.

This chapter covers some of the keywords in this simple but helpful definition. The first keyword is *interactive*. This key word refers to two different conceptions: (1) the interaction that occurs between the reader and the text whereby the reader constructs meaning based partly on the knowledge drawn from the text and partly from the knowledge that the reader has; (2) the interactivity occurring simultaneously among the many component skills that results in reading comprehension. As Grabe (1991) notes, the interactive reading processes involve "both an array of low-level rapid, automatic identification skills and an array of higher-level comprehension/interpretation skills" (p. 383).

Another key word is *processes*. A number of processes are at work when you read. Grabe (2009) identifies "lower-level processes, including word recognition, syntactic parsing and meaning encoding as propositions" and "higher level processing, including text-model formation (what the text is about), situation-model building (how we decide to interpret the text), inferencing, executive-control processing (how we direct our attention), and strategic processing" (p. 21).

Also critical is *knowledge*. Actually, perhaps *knowledges* would be more accurate. These include knowledge of the language (e.g., the writing system, grammar, vocabulary), knowledge of the topic of the text, knowledge of the author, knowledge of the genre (e.g., editorial in a newspaper, a romance novel), and knowledge of the world, including experiences, values, and beliefs. Readers use all of these knowledges *to build, to create, to construct meaning*, and all readers all have different knowledge.

REFLECTIVE QUESTION

- Two people read the same book. Will they construct the same meaning?

- Why or why not?

The best answer to these questions is *Probably not because they have different knowledges*. They could have similar knowledges, so perhaps they would construct similar meanings, but they would probably not construct identical ones.

REFLECTIVE QUESTIONS

- Now reflect on your teaching:
  - If you teach ESOL reading, do you let your students read?
  - Do you allow them to create or construct their own meaning?
  - Or do you insist on your meaning?

Reading has other dimensions. For example, reading can be seen as a *cultural* event. All reading takes place in a given culture; culture shapes what, how, where, and when people read. Indeed, culture even determines if people engage in reading. Some cultures are what may be called *nonreading* cultures. In a nonreading culture, in general, people tend not to read. For example, in a nonreading culture, people generally do not read on buses or trains. By contrast, in a reading culture, people read at every opportunity.

Still another view of reading is *affective*. This affective dimension sees reading as *enjoyment, pleasure, exciting,* even *magic*. Without leaving their chairs, readers can visit a different city, a different country, a new and strange world. They can leap ahead in time and space, or visit the distant past. Readers experiencing this magical dimension of reading may lose track of time and space. They forget what time it is and where they are. Psychologists call this a *flow experience*.

REFLECTIVE QUESTIONS

- Reflect on flow and your reading in both your first language (L1) and a second language (L2):
  - When you read in your L1, do you have flow experiences?
  - When you read in your L2 do you have flow experiences?
  - Do your students have flow when reading in English?
  - How might you create the conditions for flow when your students read English?

Conclusion

This chapter examined the nature of reading, and looked at three dimensions of reading: cognitive, cultural, and affective.

REFLECTIVE QUESTIONS

● Before moving to chapter 2, think about these reflection questions:
  — What is the most important thing you have learned in this chapter?
  — Why is it important?

Beliefs About ESOL Reading

This chapter is a questionnaire with two parts. Part A asks about your beliefs about *how ESOL students learn to read*. Part B concerns the *teaching of ESOL reading*. Read each statement, reflect on it, and then mark it according to the scale. Bear in mind that this questionnaire is not a test. Rather, it is an instrument to help you reflect on your beliefs about learning and teaching ESOL reading. After you have finished, move to chapter 3.

A. To what extent do you agree or disagree with each of these statements about **learning to read** English as a second or foreign language? Use this scale:

I agree completely	I agree	I disagree	I disagree completely
1	2	3	4

____ 1. Students should analyze syntactic structures of texts.

____ 2. Students should read a great deal.

____ 3. Students should read authentic material.

____ 4. Students should read material that is interesting.

_____ 5. Students should read material that is easy, within their linguistic ability.

_____ 6. Students should read for enjoyment and pleasure.

_____ 7. Students should read for complete (100%) understanding, including vocabulary.

_____ 8. Students should translate texts from English to their first language.

_____ 9. Students should do prereading activities.

_____10. Students should answer comprehension questions after reading.

_____11. Students should read difficult texts.

B. To what extent to you agree or disagree with each of these statements about *teaching students to read* English as a second or foreign language? Use this scale:

I agree completely	I agree	I disagree	I disagree completely
1	2	3	4

_____ 1. Teachers should teach their students a variety of strategies (e.g., skimming, scanning, finding the main idea).

_____ 2. Teachers should teach their students to learn to read at a rate (speed) appropriate to their purpose for reading.

_____ 3. Teachers should give their students information about a text before they read it (e.g., telling them something about the topic or the author or cultural information).

_____ 4. Teachers should be role models (i.e., reading English [or other L2] texts themselves).

_____ 5. Teachers should read aloud and have students follow the text as they read.

_____ 6. Teachers should provide opportunities for students to discuss with each other what they have read.

____ 7. Teachers should allow students to select their own reading material.

____ 8. Teachers should have their students do tasks after reading.

____ 9. Teachers should make enjoying reading as a goal.

____10. Teachers should make available to students a variety of reading materials on a wide range of topics.

____11. Teachers should make sure that the primary activity of a reading lesson is learners reading.

CHAPTER 3

How Do People Learn to Read?

This chapter turns to the topic of learning to read. By the end of the chapter, you will understand how people learn to read in either their first language (L1) or their second language (L2).

REFLECTIVE QUESTIONS

- To begin, think about how you learned to read in your L1. Then answer this question:
    - How do people learn to read?
    - People learn to read _____.

The only answer is *People learn to read by reading*. There is no other way: the more learners read, the better readers they become. Reading is a skill—a learned behavior—so to learn to do it, learners must engage in it. This is true whether it is learning to read, to cook, to drive a car, or to play the piano.

Think about this: when the teacher is talking in the reading class, are the students reading? The answer is obviously *no*. The teacher is robbing the students of the opportunity to do the only thing that will help them learn to read, and that is reading. Remember that people learn to read by reading. This is true of a first language, a second, third, and so on.

However, L1 and L2 reading developmental processes differ. These reading developmental processing differences may be classified as linguistic (e.g., grammar, vocabulary), individual (e.g., learners' L1 reading abilities, motivation), and sociocultural.

Because ESOL learners come from widely varying cultures with different languages and educational backgrounds, no single template exists for how reading teachers should modify their instruction. ESOL reading teachers can learn from their experiences. When learners' first language writing systems are radically different from English, teachers might be able to explore what helps such learners and what does not. Talking with other ESOL reading teachers and sharing experiences is also helpful.

Conclusion

This chapter has examined how we learn to read. The next topic concerns approaches to teaching ESOL reading.

REFLECTIVE QUESTION

● How will knowing about how ESOL students learn to read English help you in teaching reading?

CHAPTER 4

Intensive Reading

The goal of this chapter is to introduce *intensive reading* and explain its three approaches to teaching ESOL reading:

- Grammar translation
- Comprehension questions and language analysis
- Comprehension work and strategies

Grammar Translation

A grammar translation approach to the teaching of ESOL reading often takes the following form in the classroom. The teacher reads aloud a short passage in English while the students follow along in their textbooks. The teacher then reads the passage sentence by sentence, and the students read each sentence aloud after the teacher. This is followed by an oral word-by-word, sentence-by-sentence translation by students. Meaning is taken at the sentence level, with less attention paid to the meaning of the text as a whole. Meaning is also constructed via the native language, not directly from the foreign language.

If you answered *no*, then you are right. They will learn to translate but not to read.

Comprehension Questions and Language Analysis

This approach centers on a textbook containing short passages that demonstrate the use of English words or points of grammar. These texts, short enough to encourage students to read them word by word, are followed by comprehension questions and exercises.

In class, the teacher introduces the text to be read and usually preteaches any new vocabulary. He or she then assigns the text for reading as homework, together with the comprehension questions from the textbook. In the next class, students read the text out loud, with the teacher correcting pronunciation mistakes. This is followed by students being called on to answer the comprehension questions. Various grammar and vocabulary exercises from the textbook are worked through.

This is a difficult question to answer because students are doing some reading. But they do not read a lot. One possible outcome with this approach is that students will be able to answer reading comprehension questions.

Comprehension Work and Strategies

A third approach to teaching ESOL reading focuses on the strategies that readers use to comprehend a text. In a typical classroom, the teacher prepares students to read a one- or two-page passage from a textbook by providing or activating any background knowledge necessary for comprehension. This may include preteaching certain vocabulary items that appear in the reading passage. Students then read the passage silently at their own speed while keeping in mind two or three "while-reading" questions, the answers to which they will find in the passage. After reading, the students share their answers to these questions, perhaps in pairs or small groups. Students then complete various tasks or exercises that require them to demonstrate a global comprehension of the passage and their grasp of particular reading skills or strategies (e.g., finding the main idea; making inferences; guessing the meaning of an unknown word by using context clues).

REFLECTIVE QUESTION

- In a comprehension work and strategies approach, which of these are possible outcomes?
  — Students will comprehend texts better.
  — Students will learn comprehension reading strategies.
  — Students will become motivated to read outside of class.

Students should increase their reading comprehension and learn some comprehension reading strategies. However, it is highly unlikely that they will become motivated to read outside of class.

Conclusion

In this chapter, we have examined intensive reading and its three approaches. The three approaches are commonly combined in a reading course. That is, students may translate, answer comprehension questions, and learn strategies. The next chapter concerns extensive reading, the second way to teach ESOL reading.

REFLECTIVE QUESTIONS

- Before moving to chapter 5, reflect on these questions:
  - When you were learning to read a foreign language, which of the three intensive reading approaches were used?
  - Overall, what do you think of intensive reading?

Extensive Reading

The goal of this chapter is to introduce extensive reading and demonstrate how it can be integrated into any ESOL reading program.

The best way to help students become fluent readers is by letting them read. People learn to read by reading: the more students read, the better readers they become. One approach to teaching ESOL reading that allows learners to practice reading a great deal is *extensive reading* (ER). The goals of ER are overall understanding as well as information and enjoyment. Good things happen when ESOL students read extensively. Studies show that they become fluent readers, learn many new words, and expand their understanding of words they knew before (Beglar, Hunt, & Kite, 2012). In addition, they write better (Hafiz & Tudor, 1989), and their listening and speaking abilities improve (Cho & Krashen, 1994). Perhaps the best result of ER numerous studies have found is that students develop positive attitudes toward reading and increased motivation to study English (Judge, 2011; Takase, 2007).

With ER, when students finish reading a book, they get another and read it. They do not answer comprehension questions or write book reports (which students often dislike writing and teachers often dislike reading), and they do not translate from English to their first language.

If you answered *easy* for the first question, then you are correct. ER involves students reading many easy, interesting books. They must read books and other materials well within their *reading comfort zone*. When learners read such books, they are able to read for overall meaning easily without worrying about many difficult or unknown words. A quick strategy to help students determine whether a book is within their comfort zone is to have them open their books at random and read a page, counting the words they do not know. For beginning readers, more than one or two unknown words per page might make the book too difficult to read with general understanding. For intermediate learners, a text with no more than three or four unknown or difficult words per page usually is appropriate.

The answer is *true, Learners choose what they want to read*. This is very important and related to the basis of ER: people learn to read by reading. Because students read material in which they are interested, they should be allowed to choose what (and where and when) to read. In ER, students also are free to stop reading books that they do not find interesting, or that are too hard or too easy.

When students are reading easy, interesting material that they select, their reading rate is usually faster rather than slower. This helps develop fluency. Nuttall (1996) notes that "speed, enjoyment and comprehension are closely linked with one another" (p. 128). She describes "the vicious circle of the weak reader: Reads slowly; Doesn't enjoy reading; Doesn't read much; Doesn't understand; Reads slowly" and so on (p. 127). Extensive reading can help readers "enter instead the cycle of growth. . . . The virtuous circle of the good reader: Reads faster; Reads more; Understands better; Enjoys reading; Reads faster" (p. 127).

REFLECTIVE QUESTION

- How much should students read in ER?
    a.   It does not matter.
    b.   They cannot read a lot because they are busy.
    c.   They should read as much as possible.

The answer, of course, is *c. They should read as much as possible.*

Teachers must make sure to give their students the time and opportunity to read, read, and read some more because the more students read, the better readers they become. For beginning ESOL readers, the minimum is one book a week. Some ER teachers tell their students to read a certain number of words each week or read for a certain number of hours.

This leads to the topic of reading material for ER. What should learners read? I advocate *language learner literature* (LLL), material that is specially written for language learners. The most common form of LLL is the *graded reader* (GR). GRs are written for specific grades or levels (e.g., beginners or level 1), using designated vocabulary and grammar. The vocabulary used in GRs is determined primarily by frequency of occurrence; for instance, the most frequent 75 or 100 words for a GR written at a basic level. Another characteristic of GRs is appropriate syntax: beginning levels have simple syntax, and higher levels use more complex structures.

In addition to appropriate vocabulary and syntax, the *length* of GRs is controlled. The lower the grade, the shorter the GR. GRs written for beginners may be 10 to 15 pages with many illustrations to help convey meaning. GRs written for advanced learners may be 80 to 100 pages with few, if any, illustrations.

Complexity is also a feature of GRs. The plot of a GR novel written for beginners would not be as complex as a plot of a GR novel written for advanced learners. Moreover, the beginning GR novel would contain fewer characters than the advanced novel.

ESOL teachers are fortunate because all of the major publishers offer GR series, which range from basic levels (e.g., 75 most frequent words) to advanced (e.g., 2,500 most frequent words).

One question that ESOL teachers may have about ER is, *How can I use ER in my own teaching, in my classroom?* ER can be integrated into any ESOL course or curriculum, without modifying goals and objectives. Here are four ways this can be done:

1. Set up an ER course in which students read and do ER activities (see Bamford & Day, 2004).

2. Add ER to an existing course. Most of the reading would be done outside of class; some class time would be used for reading and ER activities. Nothing is eliminated from the course. Instead, reading GRs is an additional requirement of the course. When you add ER to a course, it is important to give the students a grade for their reading. I use *reading targets:* Students must read a certain number of books during the semester to get a certain grade. If the reading target is two books a week for a 10-week term, then the student would have to read 20 books to get full credit.

3. Set up an afterschool club. Students meet on a regular basis (e.g., every 2 weeks) to read books and do ER activities.

4. Use homeroom period for ER. Students read GRs.

ER is the best way to help students become fluent readers, but there are two other ways: reading fluency strategies and reading fluency activities. The goal of fluency strategies and activities is to move learners from slow, laborious, ineffective word-for-word reading to fluent reading.

Conclusion

The goal of this chapter was to introduce extensive reading and show how to integrate it into teaching ESOL reading to help students become fluent readers. Reading fluency is the focus of part 3.

REFLECTIVE QUESTIONS

● Before moving to chapter 6, reflect on these questions:

— What do you think of extensive reading?

— Could you integrate it into your teaching?

— Why or why not?

Reading Fluency

The goal of this chapter is to introduce the concept of *fluency* in ESOL reading instruction. By the end of this chapter, you will understand what reading fluency is.

What Is Reading Fluency?

REFLECTIVE QUESTION

- Think about fluency and reading; consider what fluent readers do. Now complete this sentence:
  - Reading fluency is _____.

When I ask ESOL teachers to complete this sentence, they usually write something about speed or reading fast. Although most reading experts do include some aspect of *rate* (that term is usually preferred to *speed*), speed reading is really not a crucial part of fluent reading.

These teachers may be thinking of *automaticity*. Fluent reading involves *automaticity*, when something is done automatically: quickly, rapidly, and without thinking. A critical component of reading fluency involves the automatic recognition of words; fluent readers have efficient, effective word recognition skills that help them construct the meaning of a text.

There is more to automaticity than quickness or speed, however. As implied by these two words, *efficient* and *effective*, it also involves *accuracy*. When people read fluently, their automatic recognition of words is accurate and correct, every time. This automatic recognition of words involves *sight vocabulary*, words that readers know automatically (without thinking), correctly, every time, regardless of context. Sight vocabulary is a part of reading vocabulary knowledge.

Reading vocabulary knowledge may be helpfully viewed as a continuum, shown in Figure 6.1. On one end of the continuum are words that readers do not know. In the middle of the continuum are words in their *general vocabulary*. When readers come across these words they pause for a second or two to recall their meaning. At the other end of the continuum are words in the reader's sight vocabulary.

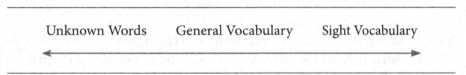

Unknown Words   General Vocabulary   Sight Vocabulary

Figure 6.1. Knowledge Continuum for Reading Vocabulary

REFLECTIVE QUESTIONS

- Of particular importance is how words become part of sight vocabulary. Think about this statement and then answer this reflection question:

    — How do words in people's general vocabulary become part of their sight vocabulary?

The best answer is *through reading*. When people read a good deal, they encounter words that are part of their general vocabulary. They pause briefly to recall their meaning and then continue reading. When readers come across the same words over and over again, these words gradually move along the continuum and become part of their sight vocabulary. The more people read, the larger their sight vocabulary becomes, and the larger their sight vocabulary becomes, the more fluent their reading becomes.

Now, to illustrate the important role that sight vocabulary plays in fluent reading, read these two sentences:

The big dog ran after the small cat before I could stop it.

Those covert forces employ both physical and psychological methods to intimidate its citizenry.

Each sentence has 13 words, but most likely you read each sentence slightly differently. You could probably read the first sentence quickly, but it took you somewhat longer to read the second one. The 13 words in the first sentence are in your sight vocabulary; however, several of the words in the second sentence are probably part of your general vocabulary.

So how does a fluent reader read? A fluent reader reads effortlessly and confidently at a level of understanding and a rate appropriate for the purpose or task and the material, seldom using a dictionary. This definition includes both the affective and cognitive dimensions of reading (see chapter 1). The words *effortlessly* and *confidently* reflect the affective dimension. One way of thinking about *effortlessly* is to think of a river flowing smoothly. Now imagine readers' eyes flowing smoothly, effortlessly across the page as they read fluently. *Confidently* indicates that fluent readers know they can read; they do not hesitate. They read and expect to understand.

The cognitive dimension is found in the phrase *a level of understanding . . . appropriate for the purpose or task and the material*. Fluent readers adjust their level of understanding of the materials they read; they do not read everything for 100 percent comprehension.

REFLECTIVE QUESTIONS

- Think about your own L1 reading:
    - When do you read for 100 percent understanding?
    - When do you read for less than 100 percent understanding?

The answers to the questions vary, of course. The important point is that readers do not always read for 100 percent understanding. Readers' reasons—their purposes or tasks—for reading a text are key factors in their level of understanding.

Now consider the rate at which readers read a text, and think about your own L1 reading:

1. When do you read slowly and carefully?

2. When do you read very fast?

Your answers most likely concern why you are reading the text (your purpose). Readers *scan* (read very quickly) a text when looking for specific information (e.g., the weather; the time of a movie); they *skim* (read quickly) when they want to get the overall or general meaning (e.g., to see if they want to check the book out of the library). They read *slowly* and *carefully* when they study a text for an examination.

The readability of a text also determines the rate. For instance, academic writing is often difficult to read not just because of the subject matter but because of the author's writing style. Also, technical or specialized vocabulary makes a text difficult to read.

Conclusion

This chapter covered reading fluency, a topic that, in my experience, most ESOL teachers know little, if anything, about. The next chapter discusses the role fluency plays in reading.

REFLECTIVE QUESTIONS

- Before continuing on to chapter 7, consider these reflection questions:
    - What is the most important thing you have learned in this chapter?
    - Why is it important?

Why Is Reading Fluency Important?

The previous chapter examined reading fluency. The aims of this chapter are to discuss the importance of fluency and explain why it should be a part of any English language reading program.

In case you cannot remember, here it is: *Reading comprises a number of interactive processes between the reader and the text during which the reader uses his or her knowledge to build, to create, and to construct meaning.*

People's brains are powerful but limited in their capacity to hold and process new information. If, as a person reads, he or she must stop momentarily to understand the meaning of each word, or many words, in a sentence, the working memory becomes overloaded. When this happens, it is necessary to stop and read the sentence again, and if this happens with every sentence, the reader may have to go back to the beginning of the paragraph and read it again.

REFLECTIVE QUESTION

- Is the following statement *true* or *false*?
  — Fluency makes reading comprehension possible.

Furthermore, if a reader does not quickly recognize and understand the syntax of a sentence, he or she may need to stop reading to consider it. And, like a lack of word understanding, if this happens frequently, it may be necessary to go back to the beginning of the paragraph and read it again.

The correct answer is *true*. The research in both L1 and L2 reading is clear: fluent readers are more efficient and effective readers than slow readers (Lightbown, Halter, White, & Horst, 2002; National Reading Panel, 2000). Slow readers cannot be fluent readers, and fluent readers understand more than slow readers.

In sum, reading fluency refers in part to efficient, effective word recognition skills and grammatical knowledge that help a reader to construct the meaning of a text. Fluency makes reading comprehension possible.

Unfortunately, most English language reading programs do not include reading fluency. Generally, such programs focus on comprehension: getting the meaning. As part 4 of this book demonstrates, this involves comprehension questions and strategies. This is only part of the reading process, however; fluency makes comprehension possible.

Conclusion

Fluency plays a critical role in effective and efficient reading. Accordingly, the teaching of fluency must be integrated into any ESOL reading program that has as its goal reading effectively and efficiently in English. How to teach fluency is the focus of chapter 8, Fluency Strategies and chapter 9, Fluency Activities.

REFLECTIVE QUESTIONS

- Before moving to chapter 8, consider these reflection questions:
  - Has your understanding of reading changed?
  - What do you think of fluency?

Fluency Strategies

In addition to having students read extensively to gain fluency, teaching them reading fluency strategies is also beneficial. The aim of this chapter is to provide four fluency strategies:

1. scanning

2. previewing and predicting

3. skimming

4. ignoring unknown words

REFLECTIVE QUESTIONS

- Do you recognize any of these strategies?

- Why do you think they are *fluency* strategies?

Scanning

Scanning is reading very quickly to find an answer to a question or specific information. It is not slow reading to understand; rather, it is a rapid search for specific information.

Procedure

1. Introduce scanning. You might ask students how, what, and when they scan in their first language.

2. Using the text they have read, instruct your students to find a specific piece of information, such as a date, name, or phrase.

3. Give them a set period of time. You can encourage them to search quickly by announcing the amount of time remaining (e.g., "10 seconds, 5, 4, 3, 2, 1, stop!").

4. Have students practice scanning frequently.

5. Make sure each task is a bit more challenging than the previous ones.

6. The more students practice this strategy in class, the more likely they will use it outside of class. Encourage them to use scanning on their own.

Previewing and Predicting

Previewing and predicting is a useful strategy introduces readers to a text. Research shows that readers read a text with greater understanding when they know something about it (Grabe, 2009, p. 47). I teach this strategy before teaching skimming because it prepares students for skimming.

Directions

1. Before the students read a text, introduce previewing and predicting. Explain that *previewing* means looking at the text title and images (photos, drawings, graphs, etc.) *before* they start reading. After previewing, students should try to *predict* (make a guess about) what the text is about.

2. Tell them that using this strategy before reading can help improve their understanding of the text when they read it.

3. Find an appropriate text with some illustrations. Make a multiple-choice question (e.g., three choices) about the topic of the text (e.g., *What do you think this article is about?*).

4. Give students the text and the question about the topic. Instruct them to look quickly at the title and the illustrations and then answer the question.

5. Time them (e.g., 30 seconds).

6. Then have students read the text to check their answer.

Skimming

Skimming involves reading a text fast to get a general understanding of the topic. As mentioned previously, when readers know something about a text, their comprehension is better. This strategy gives a general idea of a book or an article, its content, and its organization.

Introduce skimming after students have practiced previewing and predicting. Previewing and predicting is an easy strategy for students to learn and serves as a good introduction to skimming.

Directions

1. Before your students read a text, introduce skimming: reading very fast, without stopping, to get the general meaning. Check to see if they skim in their first language. Explain that readers' understanding is better when they know about the topic.

2. To skim a book, tell your students to read rapidly:
   - the title and subtitle;
   - the author(s);
   - the date of publication;
   - the table of contents (What are the major sections and the titles of chapters?);
   - the introductions to the major sections; and
   - the first and concluding paragraphs of each chapter.

3. To skim articles or chapters in a book, tell your students to read rapidly:

   - the title and subtitle;
   - the author(s);
   - the abstract (if any);
   - the sections (both major and sub);
   - the first sentence of each paragraph;
   - any graphics (photos, maps, charts, etc.); and
   - the final (or summary) paragraph.

4. Have students practice the strategy.

5. Give students a set period of time depending on the reading they are going to skim. Encourage them to read quickly by announcing the amount of time remaining (e.g., "2 minutes . . . 1 minute . . . stop!"). It can be challenging to know how much time to allow, so skim the text before class, timing yourself, and then use that time to calculate the time you will allow for your students to skim.

6. Consider giving students a comprehension question about the general meaning of the text after they have skimmed it. For example, *The general meaning of the article is*, followed by three choices.

7. Have students practice skimming frequently.

8. Make sure each task is a bit more challenging than the previous one.

9. Encourage your students to use skimming on their own.

Ignoring Unknown Words

The useful fluency strategy of ignoring unknown words is relatively easy to teach and for students to learn. Readers use this strategy when reading in their L1. It simply involves ignoring unknown words and continuing reading.

Directions

1. Find a reading that has several words your students do not know.

2. Compose several questions about the overall meaning of the text and the main ideas. Avoid questions concerned with supporting information or details.

3. Introduce the strategy. Tell students that they do not need to know the meaning of every word to understand the meaning of a text.

4. Advise them to ignore words they do not know and to keep reading.

5. Now instruct them to read the text that you selected. Make sure they do not use their dictionaries. When they finish, they should answer the questions you prepared.

6. Have them read the text a second time to check their answers.

7. Finish by discussing how much they understood without knowing all of the words.

Tips for Teaching Fluency Strategies

1. Set a time limit (e.g., 30 seconds; 1 minute) for activities that you use to practice a fluency strategy. If you do not give a time limit, students may simply read slowly and carefully to find the information.

2. Practice fluency strategy with readings that students have already read and that they understand. The focus is fluency, not understanding the reading.

Conclusion

This chapter presented four strategies that can help students become fluent readers. Bear in mind that fluency strategies need to be timed; otherwise, students might read slowly and carefully. In chapter 9, the focus is fluency activities.

REFLECTIVE QUESTIONS

- Do you think you could teach any of these fluency strategies?

- Why or why not?

Fluency Activities

This chapter looks at four activities to help learners develop reading fluency. An example accompanies each activity. You can easily make your own activities using these examples as models. Similar to fluency strategy practice, fluency activities need to be timed.

Reading Faster

This fluency activity encourages students to try to read a text faster than they read it before. I recommend that you use this activity on a weekly basis. Do this three times with an interesting article that most can read. Have them record their time on this chart.

Name:			
Date	1st Reading Time	2nd Reading Time	3rd Reading Time

Directions

The first time you do this activity, explain it to them. Tell them to read the article three times at their regular reading rate, not too fast or too slowly. Tell them to

1. Use a timer to time yourself.

2. Read the passage. Write the time on the Reading Chart.

3. Now read the passage again to see if you can read it faster than the first time. How long did it take you? Write the time on the Reading Chart.

4. Read it a third time. Can you read it even faster? How long did it take you? Write the time on the Reading Chart.

You might want to collect their Reading Charts and go over them to check whether everyone is completing them and to see if indeed they are reading faster.

Find the Same Word, Pair, or Phrase

This fluency activity helps students develop word recognition. It should be done frequently. In this example, the left column contains only 4 phrases. I recommend that you use at least 10.

Note that these are pairs of words. The first several times you do this activity, you might start with single words, then move to pairs, and then to phrases such as *walk to the door*. Remember to time the activity.

Directions

In the chart below, scan each line to find the pair of words on the left. They may appear more than once. Can you finish in 15 seconds? The first one is done for you.

	a	b	c	d	e
1. back out	back in	back up	(back out)	back side	back down
2. deal with	dealer	deal out	peal out	deal with	deal down
3. come up	come out	come up	come over	come in	come up
4. at odds	at odds	odds are	odds out	at odds	poor odds

Paced Reading

This fluency activity helps students increase their reading rates. You first need to find an article on a topic of interest to your students and that the majority can read.

Directions

1. Set a reading rate goal at which you would like your students to read. For example, if your students read slowly (fewer than 100 words per minute, or wpm) you could set the reading rate goal at 125 wpm. The purpose is to give your students a good idea of the rate at which they need to read to reach 125 wpm.

2. Adjust the number of words in the article to 500.

3. Divide the article into four blocks of 125 words each.

4. Distribute the reading, and have your students read it. Time them for 4 minutes, announcing the time at 1-minute intervals.

5. After each minute, regardless of where they are in the text, have students go to the next block.

6. If they finish reading a block before 1 minute is up, tell them to reread that block.

Do this activity as often as possible. When you believe that the class is ready to move to a faster rate (e.g., 150 wpm), design a new reading. The number of reading blocks is up to you, depending on the class time and the ability of your students.

Timed Repeated Reading

The goal of this fluency activity is to increase the number of words that students read each minute, without trying to read faster. This activity is best done with a reading passage the students have already read and have answered comprehension questions about. They should read the passage for a certain amount of time. I usually have them read it three times for one minute each time. I have tried four times, but my students told me they were bored the fourth time.

Directions

1. Distribute the reading passage.

2. Tell your students to read it at their regular rate.

3. After 1 minute, tell everyone to stop reading and underline the last word they read.

4. Do this two more times.

5. After the third reading, tell your students to count the number of words they read each time (wpm) and record them in a chart:

Name:			
Date	1st Reading #wpm	2nd Reading #wpm	3rd Reading #wpm

A number of studies of this activity both in L1 and L2 reading show it is effective in improving learners' reading rates. For example, Chang and Millet (2013) explored the effects of timed repeated reading on 13 EFL learners' reading rates and levels of understanding. They found that both the students' reading rates and levels of understanding increased.

Conclusion

These four fluency activities, which students generally find enjoyable, can easily be adapted to fit your students' particular needs. Remember to time them. For more fluency activities, see Day (2012). Now that fluency and how to teach fluency have been covered, continue to part 4, Reading Comprehension.

REFLECTIVE QUESTIONS

- Do any of these fluency activities appeal to you?

- Why or why not?

CHAPTER 10

What Is Comprehension?

This chapter offers insights for teaching ESOL reading comprehension. It begins by examining comprehension and then explains six types of reading comprehension.

Reading Comprehension

REFLECTIVE QUESTION

- Complete this sentence:
    — Reading comprehension is _____.

Most likely, your completed sentence includes words and phrases such as *getting the meaning*, *understanding*, and *decoding*. A more complete answer can be found by looking, once again, at the definition of reading given in chapter 1. Can you recall it?

Reading is _____. In case you forgot:

> *Reading comprises a number of interactive processes between the reader and the text during which the reader uses his or her knowledge to build, to create, and to construct meaning.*

This definition allows teachers to see comprehension as the product, or the result, of the interactive processes.

REFLECTIVE QUESTION

● How do you teach your students comprehension?

— I teach my students to comprehend _____.

Your sentence probably has something to do with reading a text and answering *comprehension questions*. Using comprehension questions is common in ESOL reading courses and materials. This topic is covered in chapter 11. Also common is the use of various comprehension activities. Your sentence might also include *strategies*. Most published materials focus on the use of strategies to teach ESOL reading. Chapter 12 covers both activities and strategies.

Viewing comprehension as a product means that it can be *measured*. Generally, reading comprehension is measured by comprehension questions, which take a variety of forms. Related to the measurement of comprehension is *accuracy*. The accuracy of an individual's understanding of a text can be measured as well. The focus of most ESOL reading instruction is comprehension; as mentioned in chapter 6, fluency is often neglected, even though it is the basis of comprehension. In sum, comprehension can be seen as

● the product, or result, of the interactive processes;

● meaning, or understanding

● accuracy

● measurable (e.g., comprehension questions)

● the focus of most ESOL reading instruction

Types of Comprehension

Six types of comprehension are useful in helping students interact with their readings.

Literal Comprehension

REFLECTIVE QUESTION

- Complete this sentence:
  - Literal comprehension is _____.

Literal comprehension is an understanding of the straightforward meaning of the text, such as facts. Literal comprehension questions can be answered directly from the reading. Check your students' literal comprehension first to make sure they have understood the basic meaning. An example of a literal comprehension question is: "What is literal comprehension?"

Reorganization

The second type of comprehension is *reorganization*. Students combine information from various parts of the reading for additional understanding. For example, a story might begin by stating that John Doe died in 2012; later, the reading might reveal that he was born in 1962. To answer the question, *How old was Mr. Doe when he died?*, the student must combine information from different parts of the reading to get the correct answer.

Questions that use this type of comprehension teach students to examine the text in its entirety.

Inference

Inference requires students to combine their literal understanding with their own knowledge, taking information from the reading and relating it to what they know.

REFLECTIVE QUESTION

- Why might it be difficult for students to answer an inference question?

Students may find it difficult to answer inference questions because the information is not explicitly given in the reading. One way of helping them is to relate it to inferring in the real world. For example, if your friend comes to class with a wet umbrella; you can infer that it is raining.

Prediction

Students use both their understanding of the story and their own knowledge of the topic to *predict* what might happen next or after a story ends. Consider using two types of prediction, while-reading and postreading. To illustrate while-reading prediction: students might read the first two paragraphs of a passage and answer a question about what might happen next.

Postreading prediction questions, like while-reading questions, require students to combine information from the reading and their own knowledge. For example, consider a romance in which the woman and man are married at the end of the novel. A postreading prediction question might be: *Do you think they will remain married? Why or why not?*

Making predictions *before* students read the text is a prereading fluency strategy, as discussed in chapter 8.

Evaluation

Evaluation, the fifth type of comprehension, asks students to make a judgment about some aspect of the text. For example, an evaluation comprehension question about this chapter might be: *How will the information in this chapter be helpful to you in teaching reading?* When answering an evaluation question, readers must use both a literal understanding and their knowledge of the text's topic and related issues.

REFLECTIVE QUESTION

- Why might ESOL students be reluctant to evaluate a text?

Students might hesitate to criticize or disagree with the printed word due to cultural factors. Model possible answers to evaluation questions, and give both positive and negative aspects.

Personal Response

This type of comprehension, *personal response*, requires students to give answers that depend on their feelings for the text. The answers come from the students and not from the text. Although no personal responses are incorrect, students must relate to the content of the text and reflect a literal understanding of the material. For example, *What do you like or dislike about this chapter?*

As with evaluation questions, cultural factors may make some students hesitate to criticize. Modeling a variety of responses often helps to overcome this reluctance.

Conclusion

This chapter discussed comprehension, and following chapters will show how comprehension can be taught. Chapter 11 deals with comprehension questions; chapter 12 with comprehension strategies.

REFLECTIVE QUESTIONS

- Before going to the next chapter, reflect on these two questions:
  — Has your understanding of reading comprehension changed?
  — What insights have you gained from this chapter?

Comprehension Questions

This chapter presents five forms of comprehension questions that can be used to teach the six types of comprehension described in chapter 10. A second goal is to demonstrate that well-developed comprehension questions can help students begin to think critically and intelligently.

REFLECTIVE QUESTIONS

- Have you used comprehension questions in your teaching?

- Did some work better than others?

Forms of Questions

Yes/No Questions

Yes/no questions can be answered with either *yes* or *no*. For example, *Is this book about teaching ESOL reading?*

Although they are a common form of comprehension question, yes/no questions have the disadvantage of allowing students a 50 percent chance of guessing the correct answer. Consider following up with other forms of questions to determine if the students have understood the text.

You can use yes/no questions to teach all six types of comprehension. When using them with personal response or evaluation, consider following up with other question forms. For example, *Do you like teaching? Why?*

Alternative Questions

Alternative questions are two or more yes/no questions connected with *or*. For example, *Does this chapter discuss the use of questions to* teach *reading comprehension or to* test *reading comprehension?* You may want to follow up with other forms. Alternative questions work well with literal, reorganization, inference, and prediction types of comprehension.

True/False Questions

Although commercially published materials often use *true/false questions*, be careful of relying exclusively on them. As with yes/no questions, students have a 50 percent chance of guessing the correct answer. Rather than simply accepting a right answer, make sure to ask *why* the answer is correct.

True/false questions can be used to teach all six types of comprehension. Follow-up questions are helpful when used with personal response or evaluation: *True or false: I like this chapter. Why or why not?*

Wh- Questions

Questions beginning with *where, what, when, who, how,* and *why* are commonly called *wh- questions.* They help students gain a literal understanding of the text, especially with reorganiztion and making evaluations, personal responses, and predictions. You can also use them to follow up other question forms, such as yes/no and alternative. *How* and *why* help students go beyond a literal understanding.

Multiple-Choice Questions

Multiple-choice questions are used with other question forms. For example,

When was this book published?

    a. 2017

    b. 2018

    c. 2019

    d. 2020

This question form often has only one correct answer when dealing with literal comprehension. The multiple-choice format makes wh- questions easier to answer than no-choice wh- questions because they give the students some possible answers. Students might be able to check to see if the text discusses any of the choices, and then make choose their answer.

Multiple-choice questions are effective with literal comprehension. They can also be used with prediction and evaluation, with follow-up questions or activities that allow students to explain their choices.

Three Important Considerations

Regardless of the type of comprehension or the question form, make sure that the questions help students interact with the text. Do this by making sure that students have the reading in front of them while answering questions. They should be able to refer to the reading because reading comprehension, not memory skills, is being taught.

Another way to ensure that the questions actually teach is avoiding *tricky questions*. Because the goal is helping students to improve their reading comprehension, resist the temptation to trick them with cleverly worded questions (e.g., a complex question in which one clause is true and the other is false). Negative wording in a question can also make it tricky. Such unclear or misleading questions tend to discourage students. Asking about important aspects of the text with straightforward, unambiguous questions is a better approach.

Finally, don't overuse comprehension questions in teaching reading. Even highly motivated students can become bored answering 25 questions on a three-paragraph reading.

Conclusion

Well-designed comprehension questions can help students understand a text. Comprehension questions are only a means to an end, however; the use of questions by themselves does not necessarily result in readers who interact with a text utilizing the six types of comprehension. Comprehension activities, the subject of chapter 12, also help learners interact with a text.

REFLECTIVE QUESTION

- To close this chapter, here is a true/false reflection question:

- True or false? By reading this chapter, I have gained a deeper understanding of comprehension questions.

- Explain your answer.

Comprehension Activities

This chapter looks at five activities that can be used to teach ESOL reading comprehension.

REFLECTIVE QUESTIONS

- Do you use comprehension activities to teach reading?

- Did some work better than others?

Up Against the Wall

In addition to helping students understand the main ideas of a reading, this activity generates a great deal of excitement and enthusiasm as students get away from their desks and move around the room searching for answers to their questions.

Directions

Make up one question for each main idea of the reading passage. For beginning classes, these can be true/false, cloze with a choice, or multiple choice. For more fluent readers, the questions can be open ended (e.g., *what*, *where*, and so on). Duplicate the questions so that every two students in the class will have one question.

Cut the passage into sections according to its paragraphs. Fasten the paragraphs to the walls of the classroom, making sure that each paragraph can be read easily by several people at the same time.

Place the students in pairs, and give each pair one question. (Depending on the size of the class, any number of pairs will have the same question.) Instruct the students to read the paragraphs on the walls of the classroom until they find the answer to their question.

When they have returned to their seats, distribute copies of the complete reading passage and go over the answers. You might also want to pass out copies of all the questions, making it easier for everyone to understand other groups' questions.

REFLECTIVE QUESTIONS

● What do you think of this activity? Do you think it will help students understand the main ideas of a reading?

Student Cloze

The cloze activity is often used in testing reading; it can also be used in teaching reading. Either way, it is a top-down process, with students preparing the cloze activities and their classmates completing them.

Directions

1. Introduce the cloze activity by explaining that words or phrases are systematically deleted from a reading, perhaps showing a model. Usually, the first and last paragraphs are intact—no words are deleted from those two paragraphs.

2. Explain that the focus of the cloze activity is the main ideas of a text. The completed cloze activity will include words and phrases that relate to the main ideas deleted.

3. Distribute the first article. Instruct the students to read it and underline the words and phrases that relate to the main ideas.

4. In pairs or small groups, have students compare their underlined words and phrases. Then go over the main ideas with the students. Explain that in a cloze activity, the underlined words and phrases would be replaced with blanks.

5. Divide the class in half; give the second article to one group and the third to the second. Tell them to work in pairs to find the words and phrases that relate to the main ideas and then white out those words and phrases. They could number each blank.

6. Have the groups exchange their readings and do the cloze activity. When finished, the pairs from one group might check their answers with pairs from the other group.

Match the Headline

Matching headlines with articles helps students better understand the point of a reading. Using authentic materials often increases student interest and motivation.

Directions

1. Locate suitable articles or items from newspapers of one or two paragraphs in length. Each should have a heading. You will need one article and one heading for each student.

2. Remove the headings from the articles.

3. Create groups of three to four students. Distribute the articles and headings, and ask the students to try to match them. Each group will have three or four articles plus headings.

4. Groups should note their suggested matchings, exchange their suggested headings and articles, and continue matching.

This activity is best used to practice, not to introduce, the skill. The first time it is used might require some modeling.

Spot the Differences

When students are proficient at discerning main ideas, they need to be able to read for details. You can use short articles with a few obvious differences in information to practice simple critical reading skills.

Directions

1. Locate two articles on the same topic but with some conflicting information (e.g., from a newspaper and a movie magazine).

2. Prepare a set of comprehension questions based on both of the articles. Be sure to include questions for which the answers will conflict depending on the article. Also include questions that can be only answered from reading one of the articles.

3. Give half the class one article and a list of questions and the other half the other article with the same list of questions.

4. Tell the students to read their articles and to answer as many questions as they can.

5. Next, have the students find classmates with the other article to get the answers to the missing questions. At this point, require the students to prove their answers are correct by pointing out the information in the article.

6. After all of the questions have been answered, hold a discussion about the conflicting facts.

It might be difficult to get two articles about the same thing. Sometimes simply buying two different newspapers will provide you with two different sets of facts. Magazines like the *National Enquirer* often offer articles with an opposing points of view.

Jigsaw Reading

This activity has been around for a long time and takes various forms. Regardless of its form, the activity is enjoyable and helps students to conceptualize the reading passage by looking at a small part and then fitting the individual pieces together. It also works well as a prereading activity.

Directions

1. Find a reading passage with at least four paragraphs. Divide it by paragraphs, and make copies for students.

2. Arrange the class into groups according to the number of paragraphs in the reading passage.

3. Give each group the complete passage, making sure that each person has a different paragraph.

4. Tell students to put the paragraphs together in an appropriate order. Have them begin by reading their own paragraphs and then telling the other members of the group what they are about.

5. Ask groups to share with the class the ordering they have agreed on. Discuss the reasons for the various orderings the groups selected.

REFLECTIVE QUESTIONS

- Which of these activities might you use in your ESOL reading class?

- Why?

Conclusion

Comprehension activities may not only help students understand a text but encourage them to enjoy reading. Comprehension questions in chapter 10 and the activities in this chapter are only means to an end, however; the use of questions and activities by themselves does not necessarily result in readers who interact with a text utilizing the six types of comprehension. To ensure that your students are actively involved in creating meaning, promote a discussion of the answers—both the right and wrong ones—through a combination of teacher-fronted and group activities. Comprehension strategies, the subject of the next chapter, help learners interact with a text.

REFLECTIVE QUESTIONS

- Which of the comprehension activities explained in this chapter appeal to you?

- Why?

CHAPTER 13

Comprehension Strategies

Having students answer questions is one means to learn to read. Teaching learning comprehension strategies is also beneficial. This chapter provides five comprehension strategies:

1. Reread the story.

2. Use your knowledge of the topic to help you read.

3. Find main ideas in paragraphs.

4. Recognize supporting information.

5. Distinguish between fact and opinion.

REFLECTIVE QUESTIONS

- Do you recognize any of these strategies?

- Why do you think they are comprehension strategies?

Reread the Story.

When a reader reads a text a second time, he or she understands it better. Research has demonstrated clearly that the more a person knows about a reading (e.g., topic, organization), the greater comprehension is. So when students read a text a second time, obviously their comprehension increases. This strategy is simple but effective.

Procedure

1. First read the story.
2. Do not stop for words you do not know.
3. Then read it a second time.

Use Your Knowledge of the Topic to Help You Read

Remind students that understanding is an interaction between the reader and the text. Good readers use their knowledge of the topic to help them read a text. This easy-to-use strategy helps students achieve greater comprehension.

Procedure

1. First, use the previewing and predicting fluency strategy (see chapter 8).
2. Next, think about what you know about the topic of the reading.
3. Then think about what information you might find in the reading.
4. Now read the story.

Find Main Ideas in Paragraphs

Finding main ideas in paragraphs is an important strategy in reading academic texts. Generally, every paragraph has a main idea, the most important information the writer wants to convey. The main idea is often near the beginning of the paragraph.

Procedure

1. Look for *cover* ideas (i.e., ideas that include other ideas).

2. Become familiar with the places where academic authors typically state their main ideas, and check those places within the text.

3. Look at subheadings to see if they suggest main ideas. Watch for paraphrases and repetition; these often signal points that authors feel are worth repeating.

4. Read the abstract or introduction and the summary (if there is one) to find the main ideas stated or restated.

You can use a number of activities to teach this strategy. The following activity is particularly helpful.

Activity

1. Find a reading that has a main idea in each paragraph. You might have to revise the paragraphs to make sure each one has an identifiable main idea. Number the paragraphs.

2. On a piece of paper, write each main idea, but not in the order in which they appear in the reading. Photocopy the list, and give it to the students.

3. Instruct your students to read the text, using some of the procedures listed above to find the main idea in each paragraph.

4. When they finish reading the text, have them write the paragraph number next to its main idea.

Recognize Supporting Information

The ideas and facts that authors use to prove or explain their main ideas and the structures they use to present this information are called *supporting information*. It supports or reinforces the main idea of a paragraph.

In academic reading, students must be able to recognize and evaluate how sound a claim is. To do this, they must find the main ideas and then the supporting evidence.

Procedure

1. Give students examples of common types of supporting information, such as

    - examples
    - facts or statistics
    - reasons
    - cause-and-effect
    - compare–contrast
    - classification
    - descriptions
    - steps or procedures (time sequence/process/chronological)

2. Find a reading with good uses of supporting information.

3. Prepare a matching activity with supporting information in Column A and the main ideas they support in Column B. For example,

Column A: Supporting Information	Column B: Main Ideas
1. astronauts	a. to show an old drug being used in a new way
2. Maria Koike	b. to show an old drug being used in a traditional way
3. people with high blood pressure	c. to show a condition that future drugs might treat

4. Distribute the reading and the handout.

5. Instruct your students to scan the text for the supporting information in Column A and match them with the main ideas they support in Column B.

Distinguish Between Fact and Opinion

It is important to know the difference between a *fact* and an *opinion*. A fact is something that happened or is true. An opinion is someone's idea or belief; it can also be an expression of agreement or disagreement.

Procedure

1. Use a reading with facts and opinions.

2. Make an activity with a number of statements.

3. Instruct your students to read the text and then identify the statements as either facts or opinions.

REFLECTIVE QUESTIONS

- Reflect on your own teaching:
    - Do you use any of these comprehension strategies?
    - If you do, which ones?
    - Are they helpful?

Conclusion

REFLECTIVE QUESTIONS

- What was the most helpful thing you learned in this chapter?

- How might it be helpful?

If your students learn and use these five comprehension strategies, their reading comprehension will improve. Of course, many more comprehension strategies and activities exist that you can use in your classroom (see Day, 2012).

CHAPTER 14

Reading and Vocabulary

This chapter focuses on the teaching and learning of vocabulary in ESOL reading.

REFLECTIVE QUESTION

- How important is vocabulary in ESOL reading?
  - — Not very important
  - — Important
  - — Very important

Vocabulary is very important. Research in second language reading clearly demonstrates the strong relationship between vocabulary and reading. That is, when students understand the vocabulary in a text they are reading, they understand that text better than when they don't know the vocabulary. This means that, to learn to read and to read to learn, ESOL students must have large vocabularies.

As we discussed in chapter 6, reading vocabulary knowledge may be seen as a continuum:

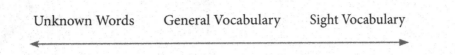

Unknown Words　　　General Vocabulary　　　Sight Vocabulary

Figure 14.1. Knowledge Continuum for Reading Vocabulary

- *Sight vocabulary:* words that the reader knows automatically, correctly, every time, regardless of context
- *General vocabulary:* words that the reader pauses at for a second or two to recall their meaning
- *Unknown vocabulary:* words the reader doesn't know.

REFLECTIVE QUESTION

- Can you recall how words move from a reader's general vocabulary to the reader's sight vocabulary?

That's right—words move from general to sight vocabulary through reading. When readers encounter words that are in their general vocabulary over and over again, the words become sight vocabulary.

But how do unknown words become part of a reader's general vocabulary? Generally, there are two approaches: incidentally from context, from reading; and through direct instruction. A third way involves guessing the meaning of words from context. However, research shows that this is not a very effective way of learning new vocabulary, either in L1 or L2 contexts. So we discuss the first two approaches.

Learning Words Incidentally from Context

Learning vocabulary incidentally takes place when people read. Readers focus on reading the text and not on noticing and trying to learn words they don't understand or recognize. People "read" the unknown words but do not focus on or think about them. This is to say that readers may not notice an unknown word in a conscious way but they are exposed to it. When this incidental exposure happens a number of times as people read, then the unknown word moves to their general vocabulary. This is why research shows that when students read extensively, their vocabulary knowledge improves. People learn vocabulary by reading.

ESOL teachers who engage their students in extensive reading can increase their students' vocabulary using two activities, vocabulary journals and vocabulary self-tests.

Vocabulary Journals

When students have finished reading a book, I ask them to look through the books and find 10 unknown words. They enter each word in their vocabulary journals with this information:

- the sentence in which the word occurs, with the unknown word underlined; and

- some way to indicate its meaning. This can be a definition, a translation, a synonym.

Generally, my students keep their journals on their computers. I have them email me their journals every week so I can make sure they are keeping them journals.

REFLECTIVE QUESTIONS

- What do you think of this activity?

- Would you would use it?

Vocabulary Self-Tests

About every 3 or 4 weeks, I have my students write their own vocabulary tests. Before the first time they do this, I spend time in class going over various vocabulary tests. These include:

- *Matching:* There are two columns, A and B. In A, the words to be tested are listed. In B can be definitions, translations, or synonyms of the words in A.

- *Fill in the blanks:* Incomplete sentences are each missing a word. The test-takers must supply the right words. It is possible to furnish a word bank containing the missing words.

- *Give definitions:* This test lists the unknown words, and the test-takers must to write a definition.

I make sure that everyone understands the different tests. Then I instruct them to write their own vocabulary tests, using the words from their vocabulary journals. I ask them to email me their tests three days before they will take them.

I go over their tests to correct any problems, then I often rearrange the order of the test items. I print one copy of each student test and and return them to the students who wrote them on the day of the test. Of course, generally everyone gets 100 percent. If a student misses an item, I will include it in the next self-test.

REFLECTIVE QUESTION

- Do you think that taking their own vocabulary tests helps students learn the words?

Students don't learn from taking their own tests; they learn the vocabulary words when they prepare their tests. This helps them develop autonomy and self-confidence.

Learning Words Through Direct Instruction

While students do expand their vocabulary by reading as much as possible, ESOL reading teachers play a very important role in helping their students learn even more. Research shows that effective vocabulary learning combines incidental learning through extensive reading and direct instruction by reading teachers. We will go over some important ways of direct vocabulary instruction.

Grabe (2009, pp. 283–284) discusses a number of things for reading teachers to do. Here are some of his key implications for vocabulary teaching.

- "Prioritize instruction so that key activities are practiced consistently and systematically over time."
- "Provide vocabulary exposures in multiple contexts."
- "Focus on word relationships (parts-of-speech variations, word families, synonyms, antonyms)."
- "Develop activities that recycle a lot of words at one time (e.g., sorting words into lists, semantic mapping, matching activities)."

One common direct vocabulary instruction activity is some type of word recognition. This activity takes a variety of forms. The ones that I have used and find very helpful involve students finding words that relate to or match in some fashion a given word. For example:

The Same Word

Quickly read the words and underline those that are exactly the same as the first word:

book   rook   hook   <u>book</u>   took   look

This matching activity can also be done with both synonyms and antonyms.

Finding Words and Fill-In-the-Blanks

Because we know that vocabulary is best learned in context, two activities that can be done with stories that students have finished reading are finding words in the story and fill-in-the-blanks. In A and B, students have just finished reading a story about a snake.

A. Find the words in bold in the story. <u>Underline</u> the word or phrase that has the same meaning in each line. The first one is done for you.

1. **expensive** (par. 6)   cheap   attractive   <u>costly</u>
2. **safe** (par. 3)   protected   in danger   insecure
3. **friendly** (par. 8)   dangerously   carelessly   pleasant
4. **tiny** (par. 1)   big   small   long
5. **suddenly** (par. 5)   quickly   full   slowly
6. **wild** (par. 4)   tame   not tame   smooth

B. Fill in the blanks with the words in bold from A. Use the correct forms. The first one is done for you.

There are some interesting stories about a cobra in a <u>tiny</u> (1) village in India. There is a cobra that is _____ (2). The cobra keeps the village people _____ (3). One day, three _____ (4) wolves wanted to eat a baby. But the cobra _____ (5) moved between the baby and the wolves. Another time the cobra helped a woman find her _____ (6) wedding ring.

REFLECTIVE QUESTIONS

● **Which of these activities appeal to you?**

● **Have you used similar ones before?**

Conclusion

Vocabulary is a key element for ESOL students learning to read. Ideally, students should learn to read by reading texts in which they know the vocabulary. But this is not always possible. So teachers need to help students learn vocabulary. As described in this chapter, the best way combines reading extensively and direct vocabulary instruction.

REFLECTIVE QUESTION

● **What is the most important thing you gained from this chapter?**

CHAPTER 15

Selecting a Reading Textbook

This chapter looks at how to select an appropriate reading textbook. Often, ESOL teachers are assigned their reading textbooks, but sometimes they are given the opportunity to select their own. By the end of this chapter, you will be able to select a set of reading materials that will fit your context.

REFLECTIVE QUESTION

- Think about the important points to consider when you start to look for a textbook for your reading course.

You can select a textbook for your reading course in a number of ways. One of the most efficient and effective approaches has two parts: an overview and then a detailed analysis.

An Overview

An overview involves briefly examining what the publisher and the author wrote about the textbook. Look at

- the blurb or any claims on the front and back covers of the student book (and the teacher's manual if one is available);
- the introduction in student book (and teacher manual); and
- the table of contents (or the scope and sequence chart).
- These sources offer comments on most of the following:
- The intended audience
- The proficiency level
- The context the textbook is aimed at
- The focus of the textbook (e.g., teaching strategies)
- The availability of a teacher's manual

REFLECTIVE QUESTION

- What else might an overview tell you about the materials?

Teachers often use this overview when teachers they have a number of reading textbooks to look over. It doesn't take much time to decide if the materials may be useful. If a reading textbook looks appropriate from this overview, then you should do a detailed analysis.

A Detailed Analysis

This involves a careful study of the contents of the textbook and can be done by examining two or three chapters closely. When you do this, you should be able to determine:

- The sequencing of the material in the textbook (e.g., readability of the reading passages, whether it proceeds from low level to high level)

- The length of each chapter—how long might it take to teach a chapter?

- The exercises, comprehension questions, other reading tasks or activities

- If the reading passages will be of interest to your students. Will they be motivated to read them?

REFLECTIVE QUESTION

- What else might a detailed analysis tell you about the materials?

A detailed analysis should help you decide if the reading textbook fits your situation.

Conclusion

At the end of the course, you might want to consider a postuse evaluation of the textbook to determine if you should use the material again. This could involve asking your students about the textbook. Did they like using it? Were the reading passages at the right level for them?

In addition, you could think about the success of the course. Did the textbook help you achieve the goals of the course?

CHAPTER 16

Planning the Reading Lesson

This chapter examines the nature of a lesson plan and how to plan a reading lesson. By the end of this chapter, you will be able to develop an effective reading lesson plan.

REFLECTIVE QUESTION

- Complete this sentence:
- A lesson plan is _____.

Although no single definition exists for "lesson plan," one helpful definition is *a teacher's description of what he or she will do in teaching a class.* Such descriptions may take at least two forms. They may exist only in the teacher's mind—with no hard copies—or in a written lesson plan.

REFLECTIVE QUESTIONS

- What form is your typical lesson plan? Written? In your mind?

- Why?

The informational content of lesson plans also varies. They may contain detailed information such as student learning outcomes, activities, materials, notes, instructions for students, homework assignments, assessment tasks, and timelines. Other plans may simply outline what the teacher would like to do in the class.

REFLECTIVE QUESTIONS

- Now consider this question:
  — Are lesson plans helpful?

Some teachers, particularly experienced ones, use lessons plans as a guide or a road map. They may deviate from their lesson plans, depending on a number of factors, such as an unanticipated event in class, a difficulty in a planned activity, or the atmosphere in the class (e.g., students were bored or uninterested). Teachers with little experience tend to stick to their lesson plans regardless of any problems or difficulties that come up in class.

A number of elements are helpful in planning to teach a reading class. These elements often include learning outcomes, activities to achieve the learning outcomes, materials needed (e.g., readings, handouts), and homework assignments. The first step is to determine what you want your students to learn: the *learning outcomes*, or *LOs*. Learning outcomes are critical to planning an effective reading lesson because teachers need to know what they want their students to learn—to be able to do—by the end of the lesson.

Learning Outcomes

Learning outcomes are statements that specify what learners will know or be able to do as a result of a learning activity or assignment. They provide direction in the planning of a learning activity or assignment. They help to

- focus on learners' behavior to be addressed;
- serve as guidelines for content, instruction, and evaluation;
- identify specifically what should be learned; and
- convey to learners exactly what is to be accomplished.

Learning outcomes have three distinguishing characteristics:

1. The specified action by the learners must be observable.
2. The specified action must be done by the learners.
3. The specified action by the learners must be measurable.

Experts do not agree 100 percent on the third characteristic. In my own lesson plans, the learning outcomes are not always measurable. For example, *Students will be able to skim the reading.* This learning outcome can't really be measured. I can observe students when they are skimming, but I might not really know if they are actually skimming.

To be able to measure an activity or assignment, use an *action verb* in your learning outcome. Learners' performance should be observable and measurable, and action verbs describe such overt behavior.

REFLECTIVE QUESTION

- What are some action verbs?

Here are some of the most common action verbs:

- list
- describe
- compile
- create
- write

- select
- demonstrate
- prepare
- use
- compare
- rate
- rank

When writing your learning outcomes, think about these important things:

- Do all of your learning outcomes make sense?
- Can you talk about them with you students?
- Are they all addressed in the class?
- Do the activities and assignments match the learning outcomes?

REFLECTIVE QUESTION

- What are some learning outcomes for an ESOL reading lesson?

Some learning outcomes for an extensive reading lesson are that students

- select books to read that are within their reading comfort zones,
- think creatively by writing about their books in ways that encourage original and expressive ideas,
- engage in creative thinking and writing about the books they have read, and
- recognize the plot and characters in a story.
- Some learning outcomes for a fluency lesson are that students
- increase their skimming rate,
- increase their scanning rate, and
- ignore unknown words.

- Some learning outcomes for intensive reading lesson are that students

- make inferences,

- answer comprehension questions, and

- identify main ideas in paragraphs.

Once a teacher has developed the learning outcomes, he or she must design activities or tasks to achieve them, making specific connections between the activities and the LOs. At least one activity or task should support each learning outcome.

REFLECTIVE QUESTION

- Make some activities for one of the learning outcomes mentioned.

Farrell (2009, pp. 74–78) offers seven useful principles to follow when developing lesson plans for a reading class. These are particularly helpful:

1. Use reading materials that are interesting.

2. Make reading the major activity of the reading lesson.

3. Have a specific objective for each lesson.

4. Choose appropriate reading materials.

Additionally, consider these three principles:

1. Think about how you will know if you have achieved your learning outcomes.

2. Consider what could go wrong and what you would do it did.

3. Reflect after the lesson. What happened?

A Lesson Plan

Here is an example lesson plan for the reading lesson for an ESOL integrated skills class. The course is for students with intermediate proficiency. It meets for 40 minutes four times a week.

Integrated Skills Intermediate (B1)

SLO 2	Can distinguish between fact and opinion in simple texts addressed to a general audience.
Lesson Stage	**Activities**
Warm-up	Distribute *Fact vs. Opinion Worksheet*. Partners brainstorm the characteristics of facts and opinions. Each pair must report one example of a statement that is a fact and create a definition for each word.
Engage	Agree upon a classroom definition of each word and list several good examples. (Create this as a document for use during assessments.) Be sure to include: Fact: true or inarguable; evidence to support; rational thought Opinion: based on personal belief; often varies according to life situation; can be based in emotional response Pairs read the article "School Uniforms" and fill in the Fact vs. Opinion graphic organizer.
Reflect	For homework, ask students to (1) finish the graphic organizer if not completed in class and (2) reflect on what they found the most difficult about identifying facts and opinions. They may write their reflections on the back of the graphic organizer. They should also note any signal words or phrases that clearly indicate a statement is an opinion, for example *should*, *best*, *I believe*, etc. Tell them that the class will compile a list of those words at the beginning of class based on the homework.
Assess	Assessments with keys are included in the SLO 2 Materials file on the server and are to be used after completing the practice articles. Allow 2 to 3 days of classroom instruction and practice before giving the first assessment.
Comments	This concept is particularly difficult for ELLs to grasp. Scanning for signal words is one of the most effective strategies for identifying opinions. It is also helpful to identify some statements without signal words and point out that a signal word is understood—or that the speaker is trying to hide the fact that a statement is an opinion rather than a fact. Also point out that in news reporting, the reporter may state the opinion of another person without claiming that opinion as his or her own. In the most objective reporting, this is made obvious by quotation marks or phrases like "the person stated." This lesson plan covers three class meetings.

Conclusion

REFLECTIVE QUESTION

- What factors do you find most important in planning an ESOL reading lesson?

An effective reading lesson plan can take many forms and may involve a variety of different elements. No one approach exists for developing a reading lesson plan given the diversity of teachers, students, and contexts.

CHAPTER 17

Assessing Reading

The goal of this chapter is to introduce the concept of assessment in ESOL reading instruction and to discuss how to assess classroom learning. We consider the nature of reading assessment, why ESOL reading teachers engage in assessment, and various types or ways of assessing ESOL reading classroom learning.

Reading Assessment

The term "assessment" covers a number of concepts, including "test." However, not all types of assessments are tests. Most commonly, tests involve determining the extent to which students have learned the content, or what they were taught. Assessments have a number of purposes.

REFLECTIVE QUESTION

- What are some purposes for assessing reading?

Grabe (2009, p. 353) discusses five purposes for assessing reading:

1. Reading-proficiency assessment (standardized testing)
2. Assessment of classroom learning
3. Assessment *for* learning (supporting student learning is the purpose)
4. Assessment of curricular effectiveness
5. Assessment for research purposes

This chapter examines the second purpose: Assessment of classroom learning.

Assessment of Students' Learning

Assessment of students' learning is the major focus of ESOL teachers' assessment responsibilities. Teachers cannot avoid testing what their students have learned.

REFLECTIVE QUESTIONS

● Think about your own testing of ESOL reading:
  — How often do you do it?
  — Why do you do it?

Most ESOL teachers do their assessments at the end of the course or the semester. These involve measuring students' reading proficiency and often form a major part of a student's course grade. Alternatives include conducting several assessments during the semester, rather than a single assessment. Assessing students' learning several times a semester is a good way for ESOL teachers to determine the extent to which their students are learning what they are being taught.

The most common types of assessment that ESOL reading teachers use focus on the comprehension or understanding of a reading text. These include:

● Multiple-choice questions (MCQs): This type of assessment gives students a number of choices, usually three or four, only one of which is the correct answer to the question. The other choices are called "distractors." MCQs are common and often found in ESOL reading materials. Teachers often write their own MCQ assessments. MCQ assessments are easy to score. But MCQs can be problematic. Sometimes distractors give students possibilities about the reading that they might not have considered. MCQs involve students' short-term memories, and not necessarily their reading comprehension. In addition, MCQs involve guessing, which may impact a student's score.

REFLECTIVE QUESTIONS

- Have you used MCQs in your teaching? If so, what do you think of that type of assessment?

- Short-answer assessment: Generally, short-answer assessments require students to write a brief answer to a question about the reading. They have an advantage over MCQs in that students must produce their answers, reducing the guessing option inherent in MCQs. However, writing their own answers makes scoring a bit difficult.

- Sentence-completion assessment: Students complete a sentence with either a word or a phrase. Like short-answer assessments, students produce their responses, making scoring somewhat difficult.

- True-or-false assessment: Students must mark these statements either *true* or *false*. This type, like MCQs, is frequently found in commercially available materials. The major problem with true-or-false assessment is that students have a 50 percent chance of guessing the correct answer. This type of assessment is difficult to prepare. The false statements must be carefully designed to exploit potential misunderstandings of the reading.

In writing your own assessments of student learning, make sure that you introduce no new formats. That is, if you use a short-answer assessment, you should have used short-answer activities in your teaching after students have read the text. In addition, you must avoid writing "trick" questions, cleverly worded questions or statements designed to trick your students.

Conclusion

It is important to understand that no best type of reading assessment exists for classroom learning. No single type of reading assessment can fulfill the many purposes involved in reading. The context in which you teach ESOL reading may play an important role in deciding which type of reading assessment can be used successfully. Different types of assessments are appropriate at different levels of reading proficiency.

REFLECTIVE QUESTIONS

- Consider these reflection questions:
  - What is the most important thing you have learned in this chapter about assessment of classroom learning?
  - Why is it important?

CHAPTER 18

Conclusion

The overarching goal of this book is to engage teachers in reflection on how reading may be taught to ESOL learners. As a final activity, return to chapter 2 and complete the questionnaire again. Try not to look at your original responses. When you are finished, complete the final Reflective Question.

REFLECTIVE QUESTIONS

- Were any of your ideas about ESOL teaching and learning confirmed?

- Did you learn something new?

- Did you change your mind about some aspect of ESOL reading?

References

Bamford, J., & Day, R. R. (Eds.). (2004). *Extensive reading activities for teaching language.* Cambridge, England: Cambridge University Press.

Beglar, D., Hunt, A., & Kite, Y. (2012). The effect of pleasure reading on Japanese university EFL learners' reading rates. *Language Learning, 62*(3), 1–39.

Chang, A. C-S, & Millett, S. (2013). Improving reading rates and comprehension through timed repeated reading. *Reading in a Foreign Language, 25*, 126–148.

Cho, K., & Krashen, S. D. (1994). Acquisition of vocabulary from the Sweet Valley Kids series: Adult ESL acquisition. *Journal of Reading, 37*, 662–667.

Day, R. R. (Ed.). (2012). *New ways in teaching reading, revised.* Alexandria, VA: TESOL International Association.

Farrell, T. S. C. (2009). *Teaching reading to English language learners.* Thousand Oaks, CA: Corwin Press.

Grabe, W. (1991). Current developments in second language reading research. *TESOL Quarterly, 25*(3), 375–397.

Grabe, W. (2009). *Reading in a second language: Moving from theory to practice.* Cambridge, England: Cambridge University Press.

Hafiz, F., & Tudor, I. (1989). Extensive reading and the development of language skills. *ELT Journal, 43*(1), 4–13.

Judge, P. (2011). Driven to read: A multiple case study of enthusiastic readers in an extensive reading program at a Japanese high school. *Reading in a Foreign Language, 23*, 161–186.

Lightbown, P., Halter, R., White, J., & Horst, M. (2002). Comprehension-based learning: The limits of "Do it yourself." *Canadian Modern Language Review, 58,* 427–464.

National Reading Panel. (2000). *Teaching children to read: An evidence-based assessment of the scientific research literature on reading and its implications for reading instruction.* Washington, DC: National Institutes of Child Health and Human Development.

Nuttall, C. (1996). *Teaching reading skills in a foreign language* (2nd ed.). Oxford, England: Heinemann.

Takase, A. (2007). Japanese high school students' motivation for extensive L2 reading. *Reading in a Foreign Language, 19,* 1–19.

Suggested Readings and Sources

Day, R. R., et al. (2011). *Bringing extensive reading into the classroom.* Oxford, England: Oxford University Press.

This easy-to-read book guides teachers through the different ways of using extensive reading through four case studies describing projects in a range of learning environments.

Day, R. R., & Bamford, J. (1998). *Extensive reading in the second language classroom.* Cambridge, England: Cambridge University Press.

This comprehensive examination of extensive reading shows how reading large quantities of language learner literature helps students learn to read and develop positive attitudes and increased motivation to read. It has a wealth of practical advice for implementing extensive reading in the classroom.

The Extensive Reading Foundation. www.erfoundation.org.

The Extensive Reading Foundation is a nonprofit, charitable organization whose initiatives include the annual Language Learner Literature Award for the best new works in English, maintenance of a bibliography of research on extensive reading, helping educational institutions set up extensive reading programs through grants that fund books and other reading materials, and an online *Guide to Extensive Reading*, a highly recommended, free publication.

Reading in a Foreign Language. nflrc.hawaii.edu/rfl

This free, online, scholarly journal has a number of useful articles on extensive reading and reading fluency.